HE PHILLIP KEVEREN SERIES PIANO SOLO

COLDPLAY
OR CLASSICAL PIANO

Cover Photo by Andy Paradise/Getty Images

— PIANO LEVEL —
LATE INTERMEDIATE/EARLY ADVANCED

ISBN 978-1-4950-0087-4

7777 W. BLUEMOUND RD. P.O. BOX 13819 MILWAUKEE, WI 53213

For all works contained herein:
Unauthorized copying, arranging, adapting, recording, Internet posting, public performance, or other distribution of the printed music in this publication is an infringement of copyright. Infringers are liable under the law.

Visit Hal Leonard Online at
www.halleonard.com

Visit Phillip at
www.phillipkeveren.com

PREFACE

Since forming in the mid-90s, Coldplay has created a body of work that is loved by fans around the world. The British rock band's musical style has been called "limestone rock," "meditative," and "blue romantic." Whatever moniker is assigned, one thing is for certain – their sound is unique and compelling.

This collection of arrangements explores their songs within the framework of a variety of pianistic styles. The word "classical" is a limiting one. I did not attempt to pair each song with a particular classical era (Baroque, etc.). Instead, the notion was to create a piano piece that feels and sounds like it was designed to be a piano solo from its inception – not simply an arrangement of a popular tune.

Musically yours,

Phillip Keveren

BIOGRAPHY

Phillip Keveren, a multi-talented keyboard artist and composer, has composed original works in a variety of genres from piano solo to symphonic orchestra. Mr. Keveren gives frequent concerts and workshops for teachers and their students in the United States, Canada, Europe, and Asia. Mr. Keveren holds a B.M. in composition from California State University Northridge and a M.M. in composition from the University of Southern California.

CONTENTS

4 AMSTERDAM

12 ATLAS

18 CHRISTMAS LIGHTS

22 CLOCKS

28 EVERYTHING'S NOT LOST

32 FIX YOU

9 IN MY PLACE

36 MAGIC

40 PARADISE

45 A SKY FULL OF STARS

50 SPEED OF SOUND

62 TROUBLE

55 VIVA LA VIDA

66 WE NEVER CHANGE

AMSTERDAM

Words and Music by GUY BERRYMAN,
JON BUCKLAND, WILL CHAMPION
and CHRIS MARTIN
Arranged by Phillip Keveren

Copyright © 2002 by Universal Music Publishing MGB Ltd.
This arrangement Copyright © 2015 by Universal Music Publishing MGB Ltd.
All Rights in the United States Administered by Universal Music - MGB Songs
International Copyright Secured All Rights Reserved

13
p
16
mf
19
22
p
25
f

28
31
dim.
34
p
37
40
mf

43
p
46
f
49
52
dim.
rit.
pp
55
a tempo
1
2

57
mf
60
f
62
65
mf
68
rit. e dim.
pp

IN MY PLACE

Words and Music by GUY BERRYMAN,
JON BUCKLAND, WILL CHAMPION
and CHRIS MARTIN
Arranged by Phillip Keveren

Copyright © 2002 by Universal Music Publishing MGB Ltd.
This arrangement Copyright © 2015 by Universal Music Publishing MGB Ltd.
All Rights in the United States Administered by Universal Music - MGB Songs
International Copyright Secured All Rights Reserved

17
f
rit.
21
mf a tempo
p
24
mf
27
p

30
cresc.
mf

34
f
3
3

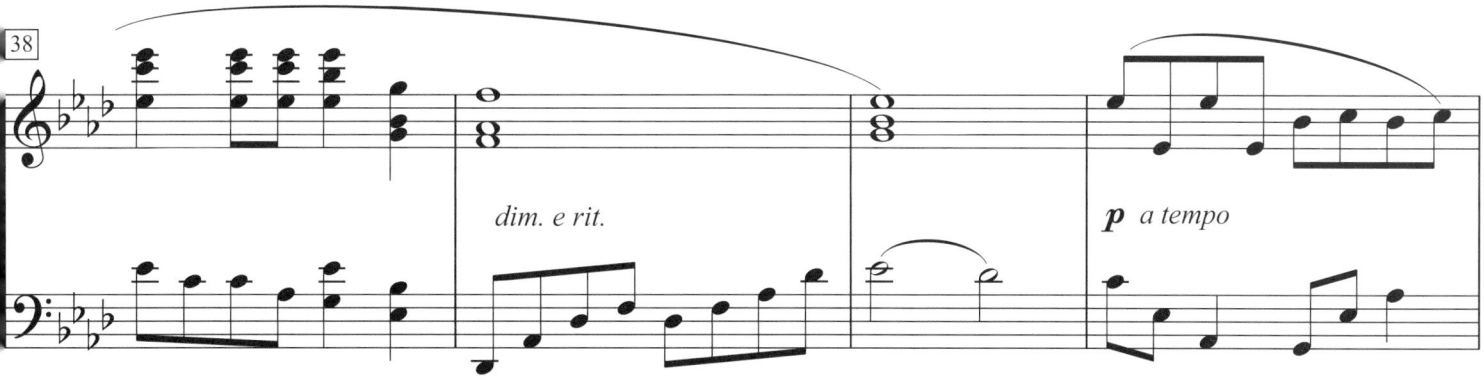
38
dim. e rit.
p a tempo

42
mf
molto rit.

ATLAS

from THE HUNGER GAMES: CATCHING FIRE

Words and Music by GUY BERRYMAN,
JON BUCKLAND, WILL CHAMPION
and CHRIS MARTIN
Arranged by Phillip Keveren

Copyright © 2013 by Universal Music Publishing MGB Ltd.
This arrangement Copyright © 2015 by Universal Music Publishing MGB Ltd.
All Rights in the United States and Canada Administered by Universal Music - MGB Songs
International Copyright Secured All Rights Reserved

17
2 1 5
pp
21
mf
25
29
pp cresc. poco a poco
33

37
f
40
p
f
43
46
p
49
f

53
p
57
mf
p
61
1
65
2
1
5
pp
69
mf

73
77
pp cresc. poco a poco
81
85
f
88
p
f

91
94
p
97
f
100
p
104
mf dim. e rit.
p

CHRISTMAS LIGHTS

Words and Music by GUY BERRYMAN,
WILL CHAMPION, CHRIS MARTIN
and JONNY BUCKLAND
Arranged by Phillip Keveren

Copyright © 2010 by Universal Music Publishing MGB Ltd.
This arrangement Copyright © 2015 by Universal Music Publishing MGB Ltd.
All Rights in the United States and Canada Administered by Universal Music - MGB Songs
International Copyright Secured All Rights Reserved

17
L.H.
pp
21
mf
25
p
29
mf
33
poco rit.
p
a tempo

37
mf
41
pp
45
mf
49
rit.
Slower, with a lilt (♩ = 126) (♫ = ♩♪)
54

60
66
rit.
f a tempo
70
74
78
dim. e rit.
p

CLOCKS

Words and Music by GUY BERRYMAN,
JON BUCKLAND, WILL CHAMPION
and CHRIS MARTIN
Arranged by Phillip Keveren

Copyright © 2002 by Universal Music Publishing MGB Ltd.
This arrangement Copyright © 2015 by Universal Music Publishing MGB Ltd.
All Rights in the United States Administered by Universal Music - MGB Songs
International Copyright Secured All Rights Reserved

17
p subito
cresc.
22
mf
27
31
p
35
cresc.

39
f
43
47
p
51
55
cresc.
mf

59
63
p
67
cresc.
71
f
75

79
L.H.
83
87
L.H.
91
95
p

100
f
105
L.H.
110
114
119
p
rit.

EVERYTHING'S NOT LOST

Words and Music by GUY BERRYMAN,
JON BUCKLAND, WILL CHAMPION
and CHRIS MARTIN
Arranged by Phillip Keveren

Copyright © 2000 by Universal Music Publishing MGB Ltd.
This arrangement Copyright © 2015 by Universal Music Publishing MGB Ltd.
All Rights in the United States and Canada Administered by Universal Music - MGB Songs
International Copyright Secured All Rights Reserved

17
mf
p
21
25
poco rit.
a tempo
poco rit.
29
a tempo
f
rit.
33
p
a tempo
poco rit.
a tempo
poco rit.

37
a tempo
poco rit.
a tempo
rit.
41
4
f a tempo
4
2
45
49
ff
53
p

57
mf
p
61
mf
p
65
69
mf
72
dim. e rit.
pp

FIX YOU

Words and Music by GUY BERRYMAN,
JON BUCKLAND, WILL CHAMPION
and CHRIS MARTIN
Arranged by Phillip Keveren

Copyright © 2005 by Universal Music Publishing MGB Ltd.
This arrangement Copyright © 2015 by Universal Music Publishing MGB Ltd.
All Rights in the United States Administered by Universal Music - MGB Songs
International Copyright Secured All Rights Reserved

14
17
20
p
rit.
a tempo
mf
23
f

26
p
29
mf
32
35
p

38
rit.
a tempo
mf
41
f
44
p
5
2
1
3
4
47
mf
dim. e rit.
pp

MAGIC

Words and Music by GUY BERRYMAN,
JON BUCKLAND, WILL CHAMPION
and CHRIS MARTIN
Arranged by Phillip Keveren

Copyright © 2014 by Universal Music Publishing MGB Ltd.
This arrangement Copyright © 2015 by Universal Music Publishing MGB Ltd.
All Rights in the United States and Canada Administered by Universal Music - MGB Songs
International Copyright Secured All Rights Reserved

13
mf
16
p
19
mf
22
25
p
mf

28
rit.
p a tempo
31
34
rit.
37
a tempo
cresc.
1 2
1 2 3
1 2
1
39
f

41
molto rit.
43
a tempo
45
p
48
mf
50
rit.
p

PARADISE

Words and Music by GUY BERRYMAN,
JON BUCKLAND, WILL CHAMPION,
CHRIS MARTIN and BRIAN ENO
Arranged by Phillip Keveren

Copyright © 2011 by Universal Music Publishing MGB Ltd. and Opal Ltd.
This arrangement Copyright © 2015 by Universal Music Publishing MGB Ltd. and Opal Ltd.
All Rights for Universal Music Publishing MGB Ltd. in the United States and Canada Administered by Universal Music - MGB Songs
International Copyright Secured All Rights Reserved

17
mf
p
21
pp
25
29
mf
5 2 1 3
5 2 1 2
33

37
p
41
rit.
f a tempo
45
49
53

57
pp
61
cresc.
65
mf
69
73
f

77
81
85
89
p
94
rit.

A SKY FULL OF STARS

Words and Music by GUY BERRYMAN,
JON BUCKLAND, WILL CHAMPION,
CHRIS MARTIN and TIM BERGLING
Arranged by Phillip Keveren

Copyright © 2014 by Universal Music Publishing MGB Ltd. and EMI Blackwood Music Inc.
This arrangement Copyright © 2015 by Universal Music Publishing MGB Ltd. and EMI Blackwood Music Inc.
All Rights for Universal Music Publishing MGB Ltd. in the United States and Canada Administered by Universal Music - MGB Songs
All Rights for EMI Blackwood Music Inc. Administered by Sony/ATV Music Publishing LLC, 424 Church Street, Suite 1200, Nashville, TN 37219
International Copyright Secured All Rights Reserved

17
21
mf
25
dim.
29
p
33
poco rit.

37
pp a tempo
41
mf
45
pp
49
53
mf

57
p
61
rit.
f
mp
65
p a tempo
(1) 2
1 2
simile
1 3
69
1
73
mf
p

77
81
mf
85
dim.
89
93
molto rit.

SPEED OF SOUND

Words and Music by GUY BERRYMAN,
JON BUCKLAND, WILL CHAMPION
and CHRIS MARTIN
Arranged by Phillip Keveren

Copyright © 2005 by Universal Music Publishing MGB Ltd.
This arrangement Copyright © 2015 by Universal Music Publishing MGB Ltd.
All Rights in the United States Administered by Universal Music - MGB Songs
International Copyright Secured All Rights Reserved

16
p
20
f
23
p
26
30
mp

33
mf
36
p
40
f
44
47
mp

51
f
55
mp
rit.
59
f a tempo
63
mf
4-1
67
p
cresc.
4-1

71
f
74
mp
78
f
82
86
mp
rit.

VIVA LA VIDA

Words and Music by GUY BERRYMAN,
JON BUCKLAND, WILL CHAMPION
and CHRIS MARTIN
Arranged by Phillip Keveren

Copyright © 2008 by Universal Music Publishing MGB Ltd.
This arrangement Copyright © 2015 by Universal Music Publishing MGB Ltd.
All Rights in the United States and Canada Administered by Universal Music - MGB Songs
International Copyright Secured All Rights Reserved

16
p
20
mf
24
pp
(no pedal)
28
mp
32
mf

35
p cresc. poco a poco
39
f
43
46
49

53
mf
56
p
(no pedal)
60
cresc. poco a poco
64
f
p subito
68
mp

72
mf
76
p cresc. poco a poco
80
f
84
88

92
mf
96
p
100
cresc. poco a poco
(With pedal)
104
f
108
ff

112
116
119
mf
123
127
p rit.

TROUBLE

Words and Music by GUY BERRYMAN,
JON BUCKLAND, WILL CHAMPION
and CHRIS MARTIN
Arranged by Phillip Keveren

Copyright © 2000 by Universal Music Publishing MGB Ltd.
This arrangement Copyright © 2015 by Universal Music Publishing MGB Ltd.
All Rights in the United States Administered by Universal Music - MGB Songs
International Copyright Secured All Rights Reserved

13
15
mp
18
21
mf
24

26
5-4
rit.
29
a tempo
pp
32
34
mp
37

40
mf
43
45
47
rit.
a tempo
pp
50
molto rit.

WE NEVER CHANGE

Words and Music by GUY BERRYMAN
JON BUCKLAND, WILL CHAMPION
and CHRIS MARTIN
Arranged by Phillip Keveren

Copyright © 2000 by Universal Music Publishing MGB Ltd.
This arrangement Copyright © 2015 by Universal Music Publishing MGB Ltd.
All Rights in the United States and Canada Administered by Universal Music - MGB Songs
International Copyright Secured All Rights Reserved

25
mp
31
4
36
4
4
5
41
mf
p
R.H. over L.H.
46

51
mf
56
61
66
71
rit. e dim.
p

76
a tempo
81
86
91
mp
96
mf

101
p
R.H. over L.H.
106
mf
111
116
121

126
131
rit. e dim.
p
a tempo
136
141
mf
146
p

151
mf
156
p
161
166
171
molto rit.
pp